Grade Boosters
Kindergarten Math

By Zondra Lewis Knapp

Illustrated by Dave C. Lowe

Lowell House
Juvenile
Los Angeles

CONTEMPORARY BOOKS
Chicago

To David and Drea, two super Grade Boosters
—Z.L.K.

To Cynthia
—D.C.L.

About the Author
Zondra "Zee" Knapp holds a Masters of Education in curriculum development and school management, as well as a Ph.D. in administration. A California Teacher in Space candidate, Dr. Knapp has been a mentor teacher in mathematics, science, and technology for more than twenty-five years.

Publisher: Jack Artenstein
Vice President, General Manager, Juvenile Division: Elizabeth Amos
Director of Publishing Services: Rena Copperman
Editorial Director: Brenda Pope-Ostrow
Project Editor: Lisa Melton
Text Design: Carolyn Wendt

Manufactured in the United States of America

ISBN: 1-56565-295-9

10 9 8 7 6 5 4 3 2 1

Lowell House books can be purchased at special discounts when ordered in bulk for premiums and special sales. Contact Department JH at the following address:

Lowell House Juvenile
2029 Century Park East
Suite 3290
Los Angeles, CA 90067

MATH: A SKILL FOR LIFE

GRADE BOOSTERS: Kindergarten Math is an innovative book designed to help boost your child's success in developing math skills, together with critical and creative thinking skills, *at an early age.* Armed with these skills, your child will be prepared to meet the challenges of his or her later academic years.

By building math literacy and self-esteem through age- and grade-appropriate activities, your child will be taught the basic math skills necessary for further learning. The clever exercises will also encourage your child to explore the mathematical concepts present in everyday life. Skills include classifying objects and shapes, identifying and manipulating numbers and patterns, developing hand-eye coordination, interpreting clues, organizing data, and reaching conclusions through reasoning. Moreover, because it is highly visual, ***GRADE BOOSTERS: Kindergarten Math*** is ideal for both native English-speaking children, as well as those learning English as a second language.

How to Use This Book

GRADE BOOSTERS: Kindergarten Math offers your child a vast variety of opportunities to learn about math. The book is divided into sections, as indicated by the headline in the upper left- or right-hand corners. Each dealing with a different mathematical concept, these sections begin with a listing of "My New Math Words" that go with that concept. Then, a series of playful, skill-building activities helps your child learn the new math words. When a new section appears, your child will also be able to review material already learned, in "My Old Math Words."

The Skills list at the bottom of the page indicates exactly which skills are being developed on that page.

Ending each section are "Let's Review," which checks your child's progress on mastering the concepts in that section, and an achievement award, which helps develop a sense of accomplishment and academic success. This recognition gives your child a feeling of success in mathematics and promotes self-esteem. Encourage your child to cut out these awards and put them in a special place where your family can recognize your child's accomplishments.

Two additional features also appear throughout ***GRADE BOOSTERS: Kindergarten Math***. TOGETHER TIME, designed especially for interactive learning, offers activities for you and your child to do together. Some of these

Note to Parents

activities may take extra time, so be patient—it's well worth the effort so your child will have a clear understanding of a math concept. Finally, the GRADE BOOSTER! feature specifically enriches and extends your child's basic math skills by providing critical- and creative-thinking exercises. These are precisely the skills that will become vital to your child's future academic success—and indeed, success in life.

Time Spent Together

The time you spend with your child as he or she learns is invaluable. Therefore, the more positive and constructive an environment you can create, the better. In working together, allow your child the freedom to go at his or her own pace. If your child would like to talk about the pictures, all the better. Allow your child to freely share and express opinions. Ask questions about what your child sees. Be creative! Encourage your child to predict actions or events, or even make up a story about what he or she sees on the page.

Remember to consider your child's ability. Because the activities range from easy to more difficult, you may need to work with your child on many of the pages. Read the directions and explain them. Go over the examples that are given. While creativity should be encouraged and praised, help your child look for the best answer.

Work together only as long as your child remains interested. If necessary, practice a single section or page at a time. Then, before going on to a new section, review work just completed. That will ensure better recall of concepts. Remember that eagerness, willingness, and success are much more important in the long run than exactness or perfection. Remember, too, that your child's level of participation will vary at different times. Sometimes a response may be very brief and simplistic; at other times, a response may be elaborate and creative. Allow room for both. Much more learning will take place in a secure, accepting environment.

Positive experiences promote positive attitudes, including a desire to learn and a curiosity about the world. You can be an instrumental tool in helping your child develop a positive attitude toward learning. Your "one-on-one" contact cannot be duplicated at school. Therefore, you have a choice opportunity to share with your child as he or she learns about the world around us.

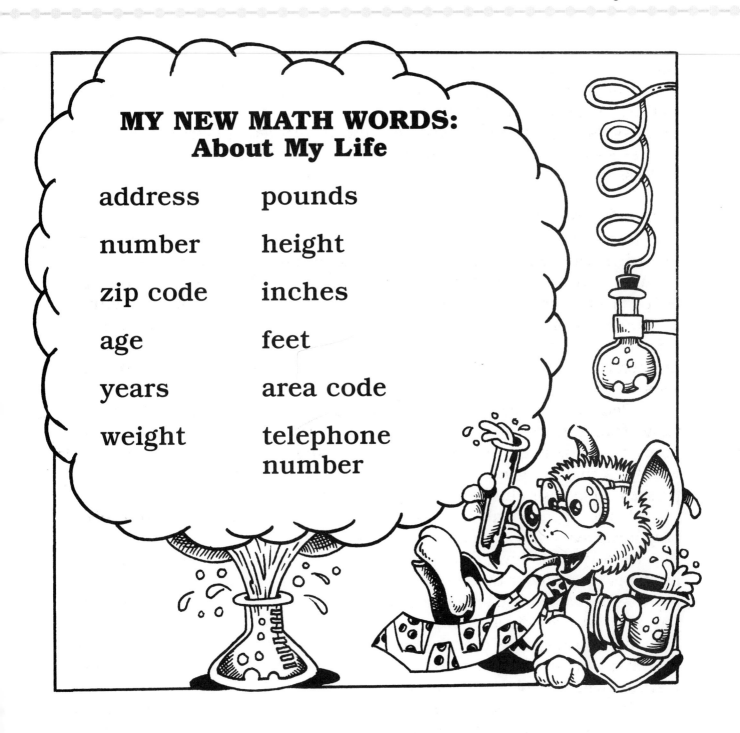

MY NEW MATH WORDS: About My Life

address	pounds
number	height
zip code	inches
age	feet
years	area code
weight	telephone number

Are you wondering what a "math word" is? It is any word that has to do with math! Can you think of a few math words that are not listed above? Write them here:

_____

_____

Have an adult help you write the answers.

My first name   middle name   last name

My **address number**   street   apartment number

My city   state   **zip code**

Skills: math literacy, vocabulary building, associating numbers with self

Age: I am _____ **years** old.

Weight: I weigh _____ **pounds.**

Height: I am _____ **inches** (or **feet**) tall.

My telephone number:

_____

My **area code**   **telephone number**

To call my neighbor, I dial:

_____

Whose number is this?

_____

How many people are there in your family?

There are _____ people in my family.

Draw a picture of yourself. If you like, add your family or a special friend.

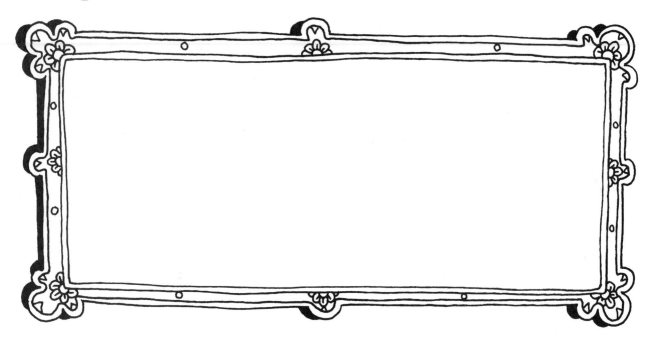

Write the names of the people you have drawn:

_____

_____

_____

Skills: associating numbers with family and friends

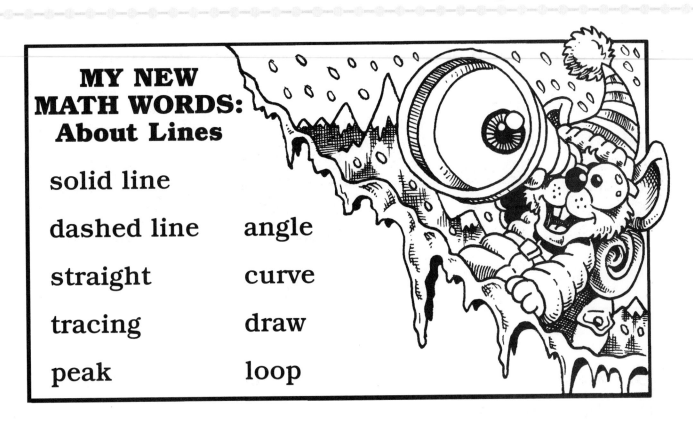

MY NEW MATH WORDS: About Lines

solid line

dashed line   angle

straight   curve

tracing   draw

peak   loop

MY OLD MATH WORDS

Do you remember all the old math words you have learned? Can you circle the *new* math words?

address   zip code   years

tracing   area code

number   feet

telephone number   age

loop   weight

Write your three favorite old math words here:

This is a **solid line**: ———. This is a **dashed line**:- - - - -. Both of these lines are also **straight**. Follow the solid straight lines below with your pencil by **tracing** over the dashed lines.

This is what a **peak** looks like: ⟋⟍ . Now you make one by tracing over the dashed lines below.

GRADE BOOSTER!

*Two lines make up a peak. Together they are called an **angle**. An angle does not have to point upward. How many dashed angles do you see on this page? _____*

Skills: line recognition, fine motor skills, hand-eye coordination, left-to-right tracking

Let's make a **curve**! This is what a curve looks like: ⌢⌣. Now **draw** one with a crayon or colored pencil by tracing over the dashed lines.

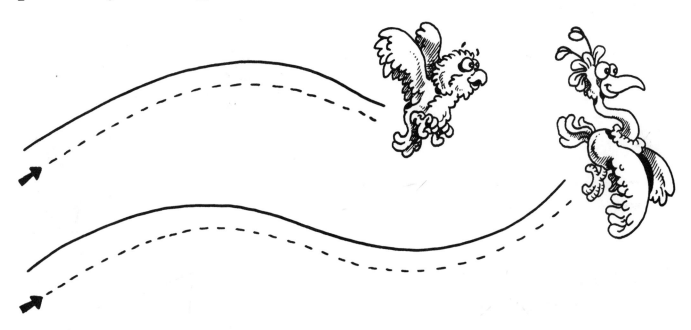

Now let's make a **loop**. This is what a loop looks like: ℓ. It is your turn to make a loop. You know what to do!

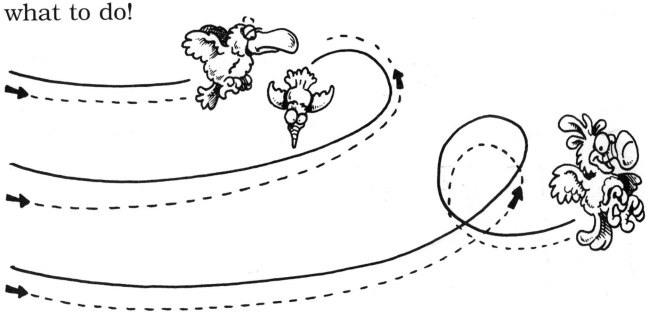

Skills: line recognition, fine motor skills, hand-eye coordination, left-to-right tracking

Here is a tough one! Now that you have learned to draw straight lines, peaks, curves, and loops, try this game.

Look at the pictures on the right. Circle the one that has a line leading to the birthday piñata.

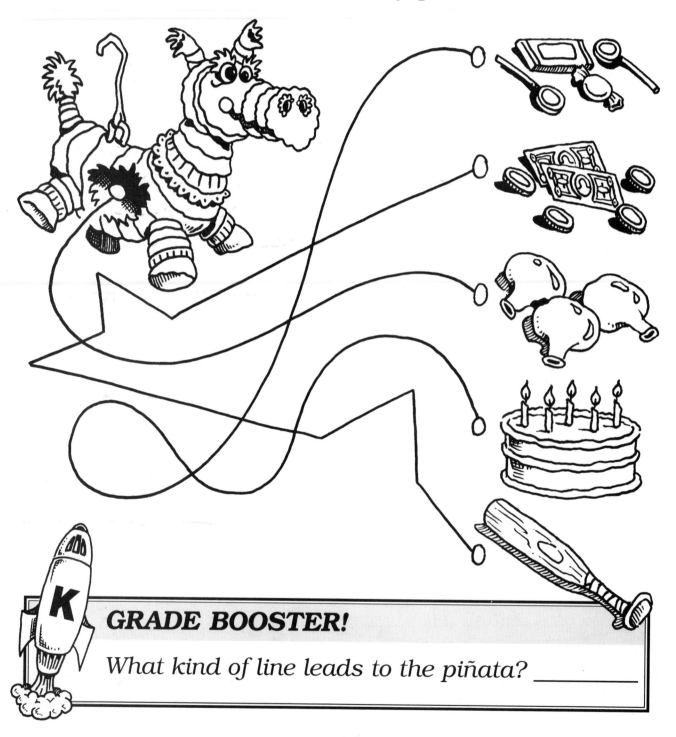

GRADE BOOSTER!

What kind of line leads to the piñata? _____

Skills: line recognition, hand-eye coordination, left-to-right tracking

LET'S REVIEW

Now take a little test to see how much you have learned about making different lines.

1. Which line is which? Put an X over the solid line and a ✓ next to the dashed one.

2. Which line is which? Put a ☐ around the loop and a ✓ beside the curve.

3. Point to the peaks made of dashed lines. Where are the peaks made of solid lines?

4. How many angles do you see just above? _____

GRADE BOOSTER!

Which loop is inside a peak? How many loops do you see?

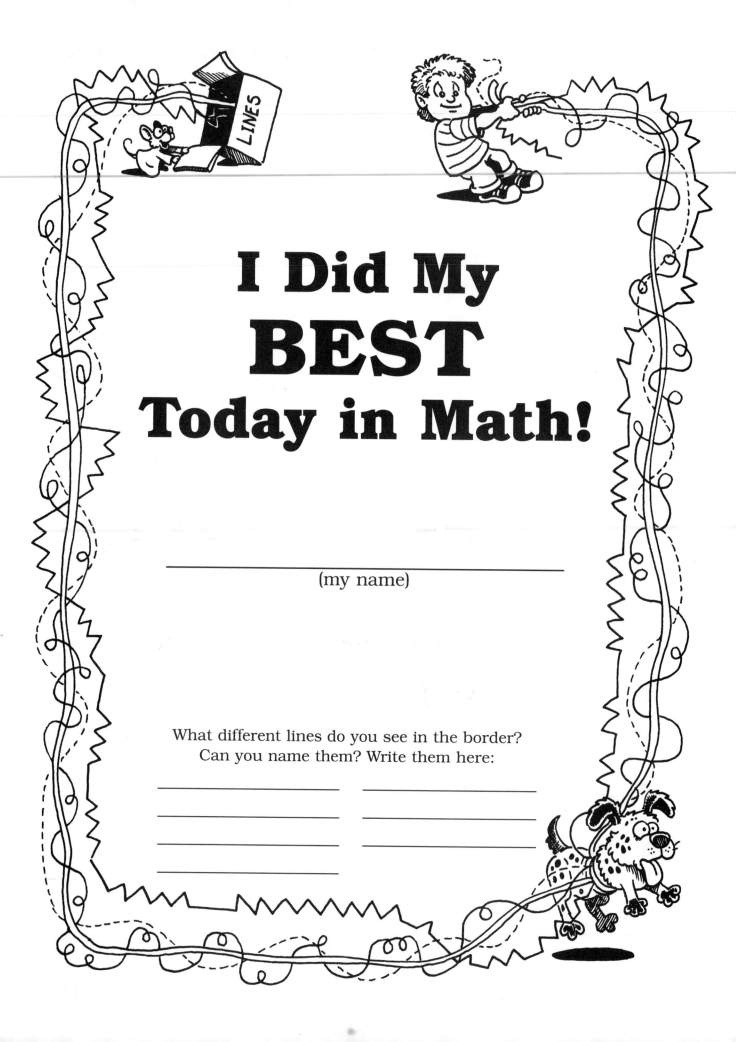

I Did My
BEST
Today in Math!

_____

(my name)

What different lines do you see in the border?
Can you name them? Write them here:

_____   _____

_____   _____

_____   _____

_____

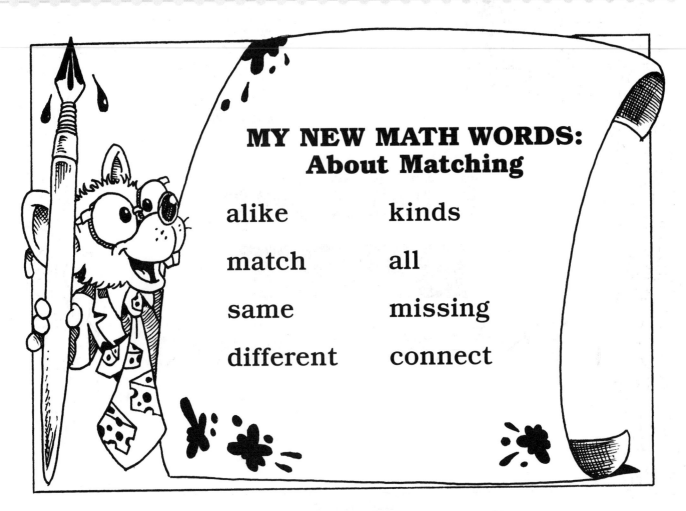

MY NEW MATH WORDS:
About Matching

alike	kinds
match	all
same	missing
different	connect

MY OLD MATH WORDS

Here are some old math words you have learned.

angle   tracing   peak

curve   straight   solid line

loop   draw   dashed line

What are your six favorite old math words? Write them:

_____   _____   _____

_____   _____   _____

Matching My Favorite Things

Some of these beach balls look **alike**. They **match**. They are the **same**. In each row, put a ✓ on the two balls that match.

Skills: visual discrimination, orientation in space, matching, deduction

Beatrice the Bear is holding many balloons.

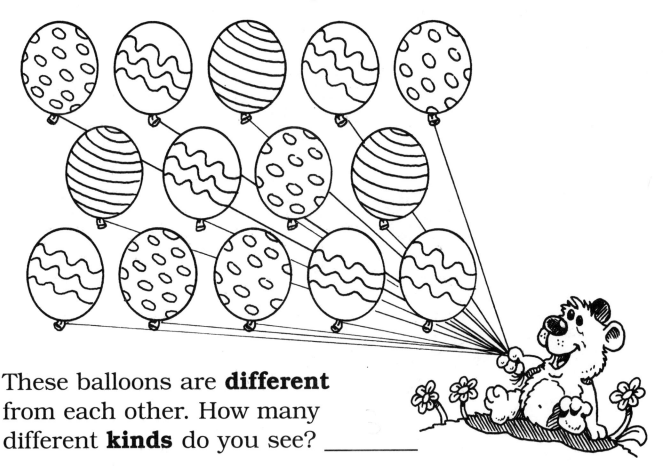

These balloons are **different** from each other. How many different **kinds** do you see? _____

How many 's are there? _____

How many 's do you see? _____

How many 's are there in **all**? _____

GRADE BOOSTER!

Color the balloons! Color the top row red. The row of blue balloons goes under the row of yellow balloons.

Skills: visual discrimination, sorting, deduction

One of Margot's flippers is **missing**! Match the flipper Margot needs to swim. Circle the one she will wear.

What is José missing? Circle the mitten José needs to go skiing.

Skills: visual discrimination, matching, deduction

Put a box around the ball Minh wants to catch to play football. It is the ball that matches what he is wearing.

Which helmet will Minh wear?

Ann has dropped her notebook! Circle the one that is hers.

Which pair of shorts will Ann wear?

Skills: visual discrimination, matching, deduction

Matching My Favorite Things

What happened to the animal blocks? They got all mixed up! Draw a line from each animal's head to its body. Use the food pictures as clues.

GRADE BOOSTER!

Connect *each animal to the food it eats by drawing a line from its name to the food.*

elephant
  giraffe
mouse
  horse
bunny

Skills: visual discrimination, matching, deduction

LET'S REVIEW

It's time to take a little test to see how well you have learned to match things.

1. Which bag holds which kind of cookie? Draw a line from each cookie in the jar to the bag that holds it.

2. In each row, circle the picture on the right that matches the picture on the left, *but turned a different way.*

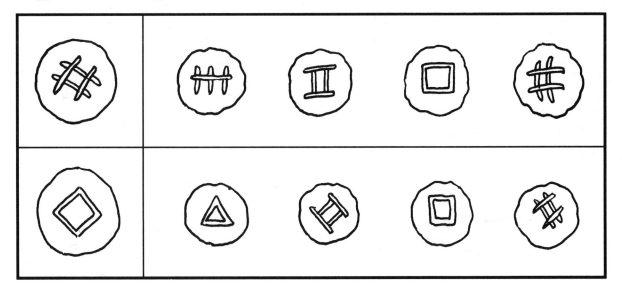

I'm Great in Matching!

_____

(my name)

The children's clothes all match! Or do they? Point to the parts of their clothes that do not match.

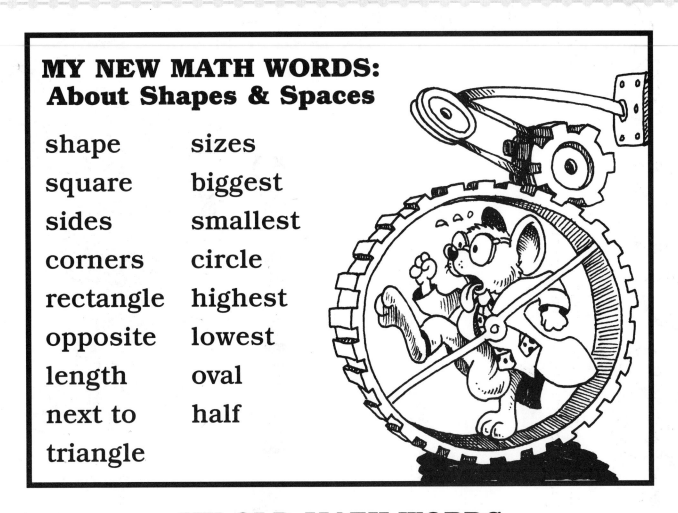

MY NEW MATH WORDS:
About Shapes & Spaces

shape	sizes
square	biggest
sides	smallest
corners	circle
rectangle	highest
opposite	lowest
length	oval
next to	half
triangle	

MY OLD MATH WORDS

On the right are pictures that go with some old math words. Connect the right math word with its picture.

dashed line

     alike

different

     loop

zip code

     angle

Look at the Squaggles! One of them sits on a **shape** called a **square**. A square has four **sides** and four **corners**. A square is the same on all sides. Trace the squares.

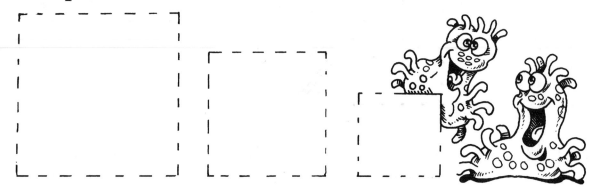

Ruggles reaches for the shape called a **rectangle**. A rectangle has four sides and four corners. The **opposite** sides are the same **length**. Trace the rectangles.

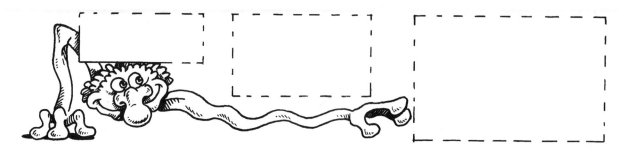

Put a tiny X **next to** the squares in this box. Put a ✓ inside the rectangles.

GRADE BOOSTER!

How are a square and rectangle alike?
How are they different?

Skills: shape identification, visual discrimination, motor skills, matching, inference

Trace the square, then copy it on the blank geoboard.

Trace, then copy, the rectangle on the geoboard.

Now trace and copy the square *and* the rectangle.

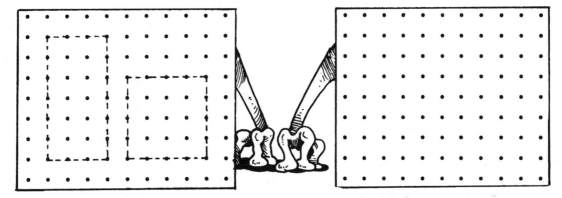

TOGETHER TIME: Together with your mom or dad or another adult, build a geoboard with a wooden block and some nails. Then use rubber bands to make different shapes!

Skills: shape identification, visual discrimination, motor skills, hand-eye coordination

Twimby is behind **triangles**. A triangle has three sides and three corners. It comes in many different **sizes**, just like all the other shapes you have learned. Trace the triangles.

GRADE BOOSTER!

*Color the **biggest** triangle blue.
Color the **smallest** one orange.*

Stikkee is stuck to the circles! A **circle** is perfectly round. It comes in different sizes, too. Trace the circles.

GRADE BOOSTER!

*Color the **highest** circle purple.
Color the **lowest** one green.*

Put an X on all the triangles below. Put a ✔ beside all the circles.

There are four angles (corners) in a ☐ .

There are four angles in a ▭ , too.

How many angles do you see in this △ ?

Write the number here: ____3____

Jeena juggles three
ovals. An **oval** is
round and comes in
all different sizes, just
the way circles do.
Trace the ovals.

Help Jeena put a ✓ inside the ovals in the box below. Do
you see any squares or triangles? How many do you see?
Squares: ____2____   Triangles: ____6____

TOGETHER TIME:
With your mother, father, or a friend, think about
how ◯'s and ⬭'s are alike.
How are they different?

Skills: shape identification, spatial relationships, visual discrimination, hand-eye coordination, size comparisons

Copy the triangle on the blank geoboard on the right. Be careful! You'll have to go between the dots sometimes.

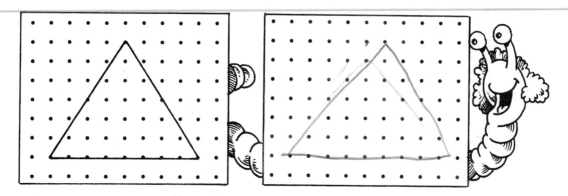

The circle is on the left. Copy it on the right.

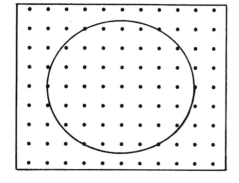
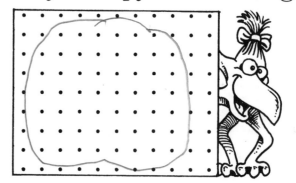

The oval is on the left. Can you copy it on the right?

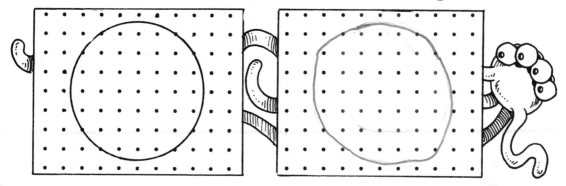

TOGETHER TIME: Ask your favorite friend to help you make your own △'s, ▭'s, and □'s using rubberbands and your geoboard. Can you make a diamond, too? How about a star?

Here are more shapes—button shapes! In each box, one button does not belong. Put an X over that different button.

Skills: shape identification, spatial relationships, visual discrimination

Somebody has cut these shapes in **half**. Now it is up to you to draw the rest of each shape. Use the dots to help you finish each one.

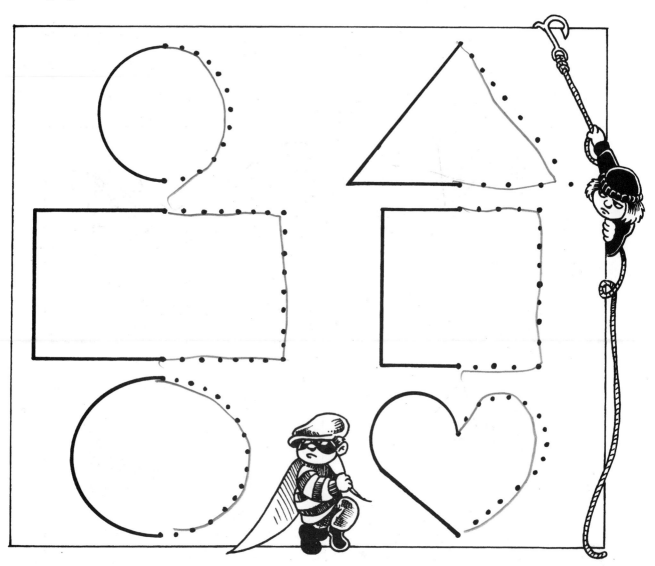

TOGETHER TIME: Ask your mom, dad, or a friend to find a pocket mirror. Pick any shape above and put the mirror next to it, in the up/down direction. What do you see?

Skills: symmetry, visual discrimination, hand-eye coordination, inference

LET'S REVIEW

How much have you learned about shapes and spaces?

1. The boat on the top has many different shapes in it. In the boat on the bottom, some of these shapes are missing. *Hint:* See if you can find all 14!

2. How many shapes are missing in the bottom boat?

△ 's __2__   ▢ 's _____   ♡ 's _____

◯ 's _____   ▢ 's _____   ⬭ 's _____

Skills: matching, visual discrimination, inference, shape comparisons

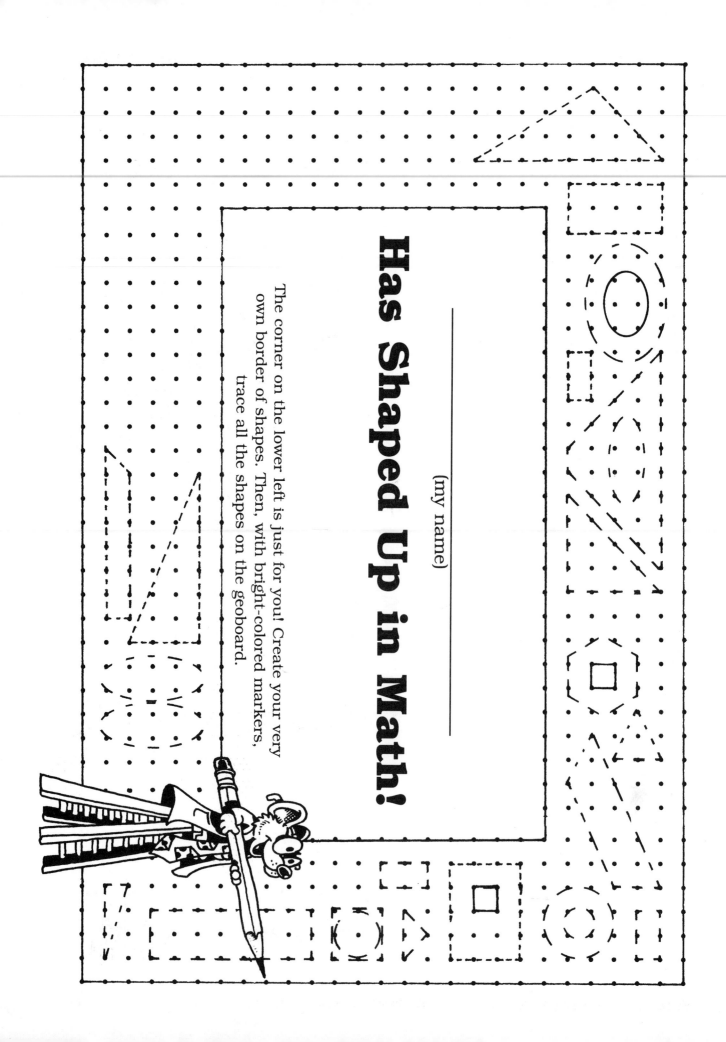

Has Shaped Up in Math!

_____
(my name)

The corner on the lower left is just for you! Create your very own border of shapes. Then, with bright-colored markers, trace all the shapes on the geoboard.

MY NEW MATH WORDS:
About Counting

count	before	between
one's	after	five's
zero	even	least
missing	two's	greatest
in order	odd	

MY OLD MATH WORDS

Can you remember two different *kinds* of math words you have learned? Put an X next to the words below that are about matching. Put a ☐ around the math words that are shapes.

square	triangle
same	circle
oval	different
alike	rectangle

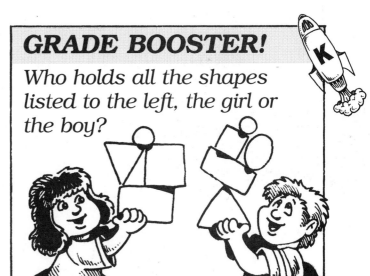

GRADE BOOSTER!

Who holds all the shapes listed to the left, the girl or the boy?

Did you know there are lots of numbers in the world? You can learn them all! A good way to start is learning to **count** by **one's**. This is the way we count from **zero** to five: 0   1   2   3   4   5. As you write the numbers below, count Larry's fingers!

Skills: number recognition, hand-eye coordination

Larry counted from 1 to 5. Now help him count by one's from 6 to 10. The numbers go like this: 6 7 8 9 10. See if you can count up all of Larry's fingers. Then write the numbers.

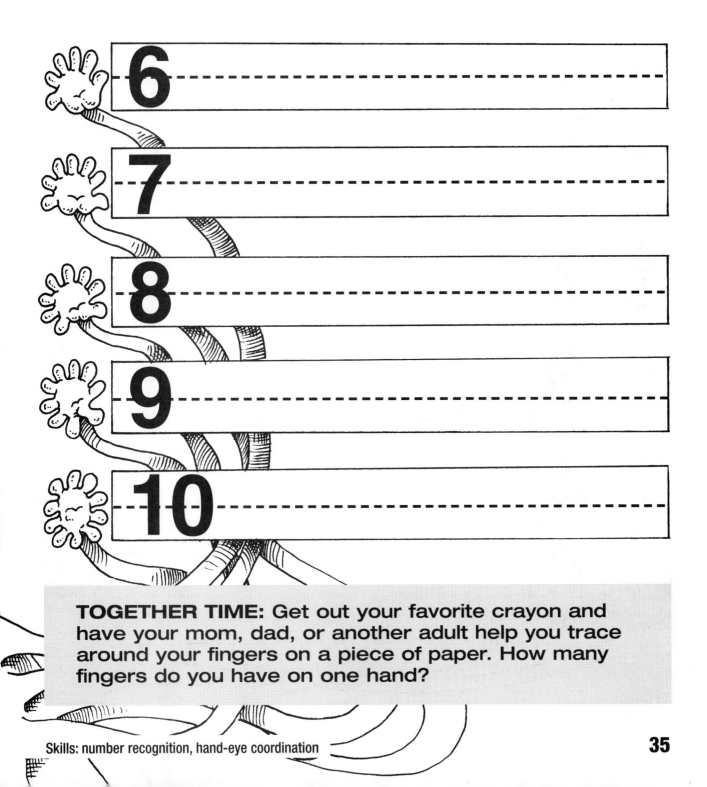

TOGETHER TIME: Get out your favorite crayon and have your mom, dad, or another adult help you trace around your fingers on a piece of paper. How many fingers do you have on one hand?

Skills: number recognition, hand-eye coordination

Larry made counting to 10 easy. Now meet Larry's sister, Lucille. She has even more fingers than Larry! She'll help you learn to count from 11 to 15. Count her fingers and write, write, write!

11

12

13

14

15

GRADE BOOSTER!

When you and a friend are riding together in a car or bus, count the number of trees or houses you pass by. Happy counting!

Skills: number recognition, hand-eye coordination

Lucky for Lucille that she has lots of hands—she can count from 16 to 20. You can help her! Count her fingers and write the numbers.

TOGETHER TIME: How many of your own handprints do you need to count to ten? _____ Fifteen? _____ How about twenty? _____ How about thirty? _____ How about . . . ?

Oh, no, some numbers are **missing**! As you count from 1 to 10, write in the missing numbers:

More missing numbers! As you count from 11 to 20, write in the numbers that have disappeared.

GRADE BOOSTER!

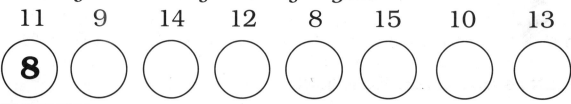

*When you can write down numbers without skipping any or jumbling them up, you have written them **in order**. The numbers below are mixed up. Put them in the circles in the right order. The first one is filled in for you.*

11   9   14   12   8   15   10   13

(8) ( ) ( ) ( ) ( ) ( ) ( ) ( )

Skills: number recognition, number sequencing, hand-eye coordination

Oscar the Owl is a strange bird—he has lines and numbers on his feathers. On the blank lines, write the numbers that come **before** and **after** the number written.

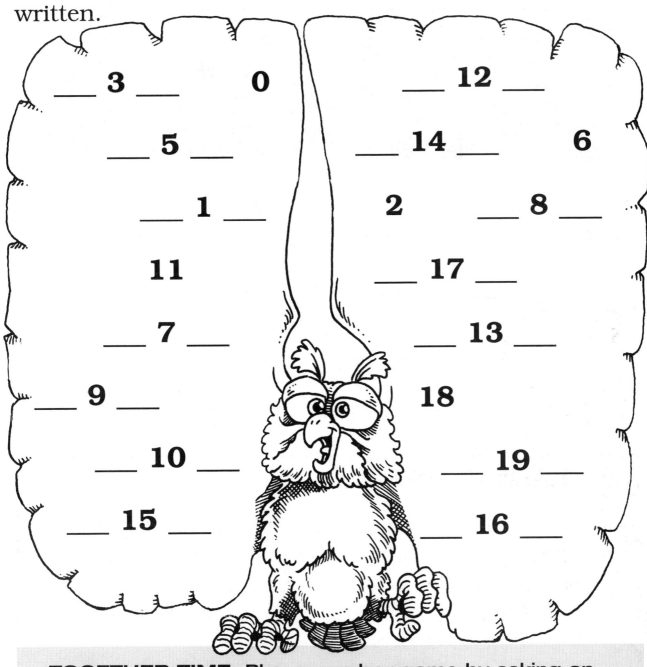

__ 3 __   0

__ 5 __

__ 1 __

11

__ 7 __

__ 9 __

__ 10 __

__ 15 __

__ 12 __

__ 14 __   6

2   __ 8 __

__ 17 __

__ 13 __

18

__ 19 __

__ 16 __

TOGETHER TIME: Play a number game by asking an adult to write down a number between 1 and 20. Now it's your turn to write down the numbers that come before and after. Play again!

Skills: number recognition, number sequencing, ordering, inference, deduction

39

Can you count the BIG numbers below? They are called **even** numbers. When you count even numbers, you are counting by **two's**.

₁**2**₃**4**₅**6**₇**8**₉**10**₁₁**12**₁₃**14**₁₅**16**₁₇**18**₁₉**20**

Where are the even numbers? Are they in the apples or the pears? Circle where the even numbers are: Now count the even numbers out loud.

Now that you know the even numbers, help Cindy the Centipede fill in the missing even numbers:

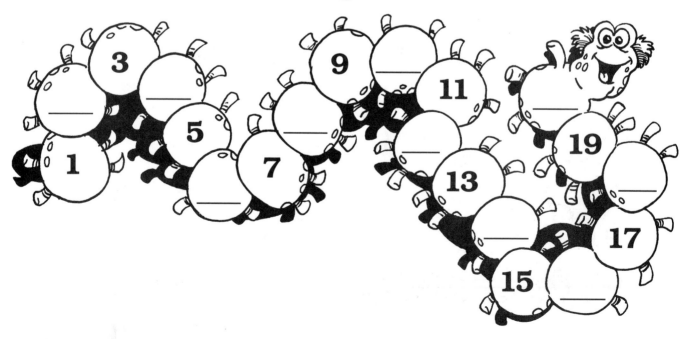

Skills: number recognition, even numbering, counting by two's

Here are more BIG numbers. But these aren't *even* numbers. They're **odd** numbers. They come **between** the even ones.

1 ₂**3** ₄**5** ₆**7** ₈**9** ₁₀**11** ₁₂**13** ₁₄**15** ₁₆**17** ₁₈**19** ₂₀

Where are the odd numbers? They can't be in the apples, because that's where the even numbers are. Circle where the odd numbers must be:
Now count the odd numbers out loud.

Now help Mookie the Monkey fill in the missing odd numbers:

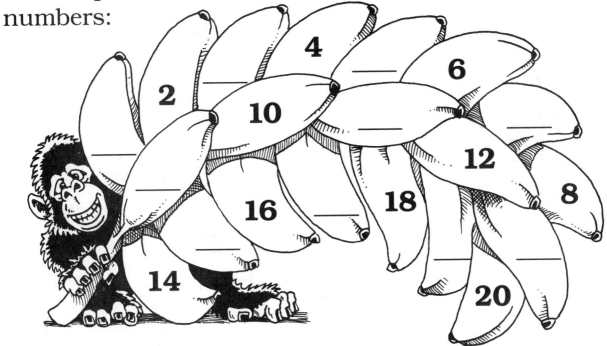

Skills: number recognition, odd numbering, counting by two's

This is the way we count numbers by **five's** from 1 to 25:

1 2 3 4 **5** 6 7 8 9 **10** 11 12 13 14 **15** 16 17 18 19 **20** 21 22 23 24 **25**

Can you count by five's? Write the missing numbers in the presents.

Below are the dalmatian twins. Can you find out how many spots they have? (*Hint:* Count by five's to find the answer!)

TOGETHER TIME: What do you suppose would be a good name for the dalmatian twins? Together with an adult, come up with names for your two spotty pals. Write them here:

_____   _____

Skills: number recognition, counting by five's

Kurly Kangaroo has jumbled up some numbers. Help him put the numbers in the large shapes in order, from **least** to **greatest**. Write them in the smaller shapes. The first row is started for you.

LET'S REVIEW

How much have you learned about numbers and counting? The following test is a tough one. Jack the Juggler has mixed up his circles, triangles, and squares and is missing some numbers.

1. Count by two's to see which even numbers are missing. Fill in the empty ◯'s *only.*

2. Count by two's to find out which odd numbers are missing. Fill in empty △'s *only.*

3. Count by five's to find out which other numbers are still missing. Fill in the empty ☐'s.

I Am a Super Number Counter!

_____
(my name)

Which odd numbers are missing? Which even ones?
How about five's? How many baby chicks do you see?

MY NEW MATH WORDS: About Positions

position
left
right
front
back
middle
top
bottom
inside
on
outside

MY OLD MATH WORDS

Now that you know how to count, how many old math words do you see? _____ How many are about counting? _____

area code	two's	weight	square
zip code	number	years	odd
five's	even	loop	tracing
one's	ten's	count	after

Skills: math literacy, vocabulary building, counting

When we talk about where different things are, especially when compared to each other, we are talking about **position**. Now that you know what position means, let's go exploring!

This bird is on the **left** . . .

. . . and this one is on the **right**.

This explorer is pointing left . . .

. . . and this one is pointing right.

TOGETHER TIME: Ask your mom, dad, or a friend to play a game with you. Have them point to the animals above, one by one. With each animal, you say whether there's another animal to the left or right of the first animal. Also say who is in **front** and who is in **back** of that animal.

Skills: understanding directions, locating positions

I Know Where Things Are

These astronauts are space walking above the planet of Wheresville. Circle the one who is in the **middle**.

These astronauts have blasted off the surface of Wheresville in their spaceship. Circle the one who is in the middle.

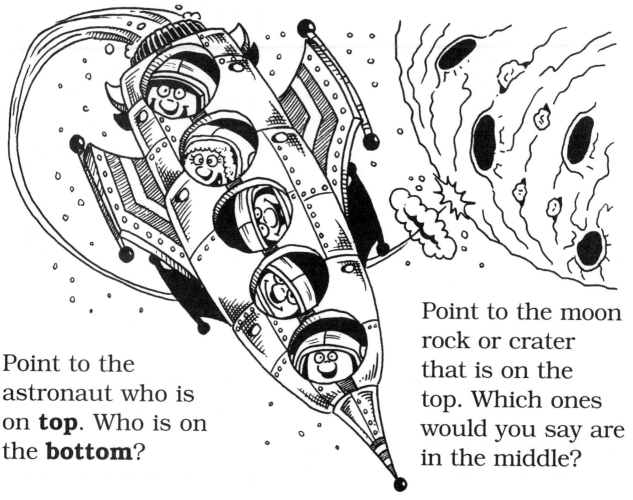

Point to the astronaut who is on **top**. Who is on the **bottom**?

Point to the moon rock or crater that is on the top. Which ones would you say are in the middle?

Skills: understanding directions, locating and differentiating positions

There's the gate to the zoo! It's a strange-looking gate, isn't it? The triangle is **inside** the circle. The square is **on** the circle, and the rectangle is **outside** the circle.

You are outside the zoo. Open the gate and walk inside!

Circle all the animals outside the fence. Two birds are on the fence. Put a ✔ beside them.

Some animals are inside the fence. Put a small X next to them.

GRADE BOOSTER!

How many animals are outside the fence? _____
How many are inside? _____ Is the bird flying
inside or outside the fence?

LET'S REVIEW

If you can finish this test, you really know where things are! Use the directions to fill in the names of the people in Maria's family on the lines below. Maria has two brothers and two sisters.

1. Maria is on the top.

2. José is to the left of Carlos.

3. Alicia is to the right of Tina.

4. Who is who? Fill in the names.

 _____

 _____

 _____

 _____

_____

Skills: spatial discrimination, understanding directions, locating and differentiating positions

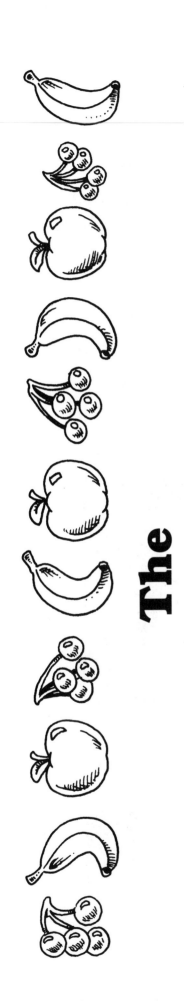

The
"I Know Where Things Are"
Award Is Presented to:

_____

(my name)

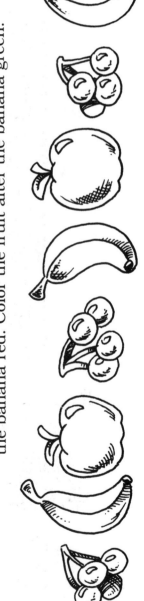

Have some more fun! Color the fruit to the right of the cherries yellow. Color the fruit to the left of the banana red. Color the fruit after the banana green.

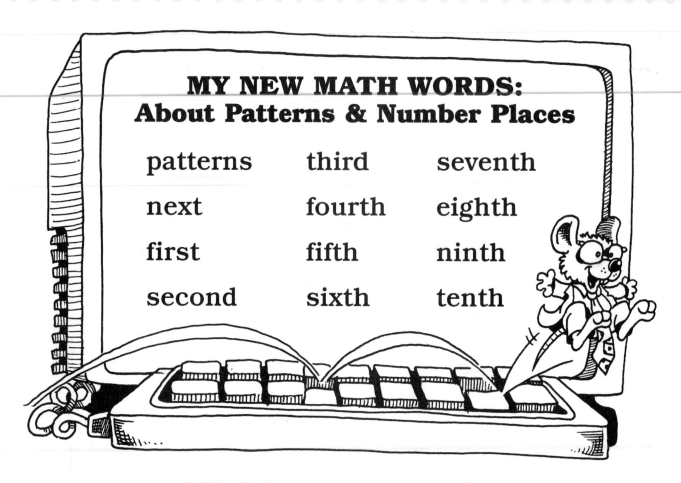

MY OLD MATH WORDS

The columns in the box are labeled LEFT, MIDDLE, and RIGHT. In which column are the old math words about counting numbers?

Now point to the old math words about yourself. Are they in the LEFT, MIDDLE, or RIGHT column?

⇦ LEFT	⇦ MIDDLE ⇨	RIGHT ⇨
5 years old	triangle	one
555-6724	circle	two
127 Olive St.	square	five
52 pounds	oval	ten

Point to the old math words about shapes. Are they in the LEFT column? In the MIDDLE? Or the RIGHT?

Skills: visual discrimination, understanding relationships, sequencing

Patterns are fun to find! In each row, put a ✓ next to the box with the shape that comes **next** in the pattern.

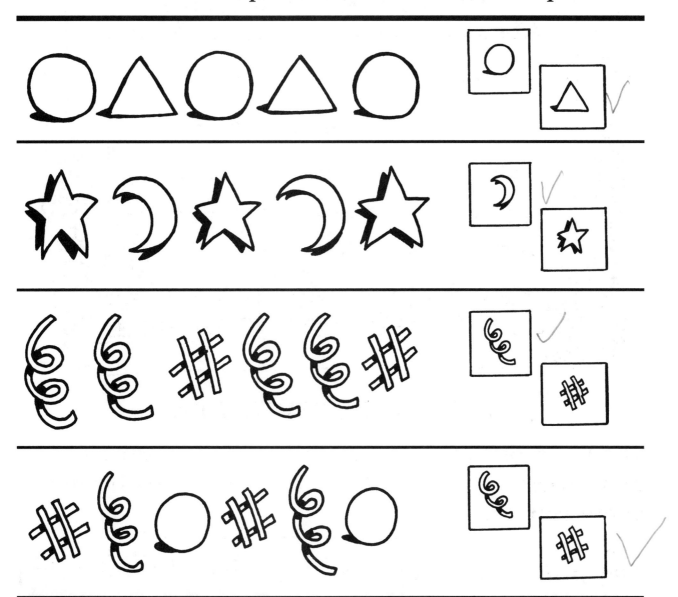

GRADE BOOSTER!

Draw your own pattern using ◯'s, △'s, and ▢'s.

Circle the box with the face that comes next in the pattern.

Example:

Skills: patterns, visual discrimination, sequencing, inference

Which box on the right has all the shapes in the necklace Miss Petunia is wearing? Cross out the boxes that do *not* contain all the correct shapes.

Help Farmer Bill find the patterns that match. For each garden plot, put a ✓ next to the two rows of vegetables that have a matching pattern.

Example:

Skills: patterns, visual discrimination, sequencing, matching, inference

GRADE BOOSTER!

Help Rita Rabbit find her friends in the carrot patch. They are hiding in two special patterns in the garden. Find the patterns. Then color them two different colors.

How are the two patterns different?

Now create your very own bunny pattern using spots, stripes, anything you want!

Skills: patterns, visual discrimination, sequencing, inference

It's fun to make music together, especially on drums with colorful patterns on them! Color the short drum as follows: △'s RED, ▭'s YELLOW, ○'s BLUE.

Then make your own pattern on the tall drum. Use △'s, ▭'s, and ○'s. Be sure to create a repeating pattern.

How will you color the dancing dog's mask?

Skills: patterns, visual discrimination, sequencing and ordering

This is the way we put things in order: by numbering them from left to right. Everyone has a special place in line.

| **first** | **second** | **third** | **fourth** | **fifth** | **sixth** |
| 1st | 2nd | 3rd | 4th | 5th | 6th |

In each of the boxes below, circle the correct place each person has in line. The first one is done for you.

1st **(2nd)** 3rd	2nd 3rd 4th
1st 3rd 5th	3rd 4th 5th
2nd 3rd 4th	2nd 4th 6th

Skills: ordinals, visual discrimination, sequencing and ordering

On your mark, get set, go! The animals in the car are racing to the finish line, but they are missing their numbers! Pick a number from the Number Box to go on each racing shirt. The numbers need to be in order. The first one is done for you.

Number Box

third/3rd   sixth/6th
fourth/4th   fifth/5th
ninth/9th
seventh/7th
second/2nd
eighth/8th
tenth/10th

GRADE BOOSTER!

Create a pattern of color in the racers! Every other racer is yellow. The racers in between are red.

Skills: ordinals, visual discrimination, sequencing and ordering, odd and even numbers

LET'S REVIEW

Here's a little test to see how much you have learned about patterns and numbers.

1. Which comes next in the pattern? Circle it.

 or

2. Which number comes next in the pattern? Circle it.

1 2 3 1 2 3 1   1 or 2 or 3

3. Who is third in line? Put a circle around him or her. Which kid is fifth in line? Put a ✓ next to him or her.

GRADE BOOSTER!

You can create a color pattern in the row of marching kids! Color the first marcher green, the second one yellow, and the third one blue. Then repeat the pattern. How many times does the pattern repeat?

I Earned a

1ST

Place in

Patterns

& Numbers!

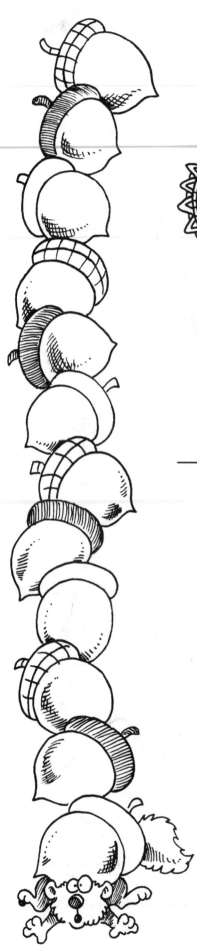

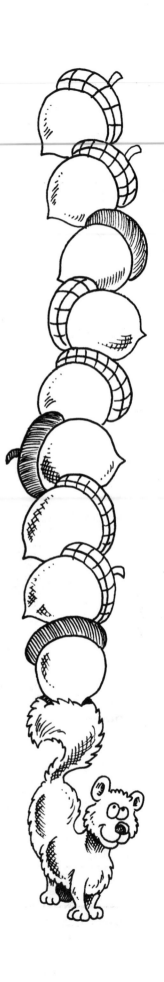

_____
(my name)

Number both piles of acorns in order,
starting with the bottom acorn.

Which squirrel holds acorns
patterned like this?

How many times does this
pattern repeat?

_____

Answers

page 10 GB: There are seven dashed angles.

page 12 GB: A *curved* line leads from the balloons to the piñata.

page 13 1. ✓ 2. ✓ 3. Solid lines are on left. Dashed lines are on right.
4. There are 24 angles.
GB: There are 4 loops.

page 16

page 17 There are 3 different kinds of balloons.
There are 6 's, 5 's, and 3 's.

page 18

page 19

page 20 GB:
elephant—peanuts;
giraffe—leaves;
mouse —cheese;
horse—hay;
bunny—carrots

page 21 1.   2.

page 23 dashed line— ; alike— ;
different— ; loop— ;
zip code— 91505; angle—

page 24

page 26 GB: purple
blue   orange   green

page 27 There are 3 angles in a triangle. There
are 2 squares and 8 triangles in the box.

page 29

page 31 1.   2. There are 2 △'s,
3 ▭'s,
2 ♡'s, 3 ◯'s,
1 ▯, and
3 ⬭'s.

page 33 Shapes—*square, triangle, circle, oval, rectangle.* Matching words—*same, alike, different.*
GB: The boy holds all the shapes listed.

page 37 TT: Two handprints are needed to count to 10. Three are needed for 15, four for 20,
and six for 30.

page 38 Missing numbers on children's T-shirts are 3, 5, 8, and 9.
Missing numbers in rollerblades are 12, 14, 17, and 20.
GB: 8, 9, 10, 11, 12, 13, 14, and 15.

Answers

page 39

page 40 The even numbers are in the 🍎.

page 41 The odd numbers are in the 🍐.

page 42

Each twin has 20 spots on its face.

page 43
1st row: 3, 4, 7, 8, 9, 10;
2nd row: 2, 5, 6, 10, 11, 12, 14;
3rd row: 13, 17, 18, 19, 21, 23

page 44 1. 8, 12, 14, and 18 are missing. 2. 3, 9, and 17 are missing. 3. 5, 15, and 20 are missing.

page 46 There are 16 old math words listed at the bottom of the page. Eight are about counting.

page 48

page 49

Three animals are outside the fence. Four animals are inside the fence. The bird is flying *over* the fence.

page 50 Maria José Carlos Tina Alicia

page 52 Math words about counting are in the RIGHT column. Math words about yourself are in the LEFT column. Math words about shapes are in the MIDDLE.

page 53 Row 1: △ Row 2: ☽ Row 3: 🖎 Row 4: 🎑

page 54 Row 1: 🐵 Row 2: 🐵 Row 3: 🐵 Row 4: 🐵

page 56

page 55 The lowest box contains all the correct shapes.

page 57 The first and third rows of bunnies match—the pattern is two spotted bunnies, one white bunny. The second and fourth rows of bunnies match—the pattern is every other bunny is white, then spotted.

page 59 Doctor—2nd; firefighter—1st; plumber—3rd; teacher—4th; police officer—5th; dentist—6th.

page 60

page 61 1. 🐻 2. **2**

3. The boy on the right is leading the line and is first.

GB: The pattern repeats three times.